POWERFUL
SPEAKING

THE FIVE-STEP PLAN TO MASTERING YOUR SPEECH OR PRESENTATION

Tom Duncan

For the courageous

Contents

Introduction

Why did you pick up this book? Chances are that you have an impending public speaking event and, if you are like most people, the prospect of that fills you with dread. Perhaps you have had a negative experience of speaking in public and you want to improve on it next time. Or perhaps your fear of public speaking is starting to hold you back at work because you are avoiding opportunities to present. Whatever drove you pick it up - welcome dear reader, you have come to the right place.

The good news is that anyone can learn to be a master public speaker. And I mean anyone. Public speaking is not some innate skill that some people are born with and are others not. Everyone has the ability within them to become a magnificent public speaker. Yes, even you. The even better news is that improving your public speaking will change every aspect of your life too. It will improve your personal and professional relationships. It will improve your confidence. It will make you happier. I am not exaggerating.

At its most basic, public speaking is about communication. Every time you open your mouth, or every time you decide not to, you are using communication skills. A business meeting is a public speaking engagement. A chat with your barista is a public speaking engagement. A phone conversation with your best friend or partner is a public speaking engagement. Because every single conversation you have is a public speaking engagement, the journey of self-improvement that you have just begun by picking up this book will bring positive ramifications for your life that you cannot even imagine. I know, it did so for me and countless other novice speakers I have worked with over the years. As you deepen your skills through practice and experience you will be amazed at the improvements you will gain.

The fact that most people are so fearful of public speaking is an advantage. It means that when you develop your own skills you will already be ahead of the majority of the population who are held back by their fear and do nothing to overcome it. When you learn that you can take on high-profile speaking roles and excel you will be amongst the tiny minority of people who have discovered the secret that the transformational power of speaking is accessible to anyone. And it will change your life. Think of the possibilities that will open up.

Public speaking is part science, part art. This book will teach you the science part, which involves putting certain processes and techniques into practice in the preparation and delivery of your speeches. These processes and techniques are tried and tested ways in which to deliver effective talks, proven through the thousands of successful talks I have witnessed from all types of people delivering all types of speeches in all types of settings. Applying these techniques and processes will ensure that you achieve your objectives every single time, whether it is to deliver a wedding speech, a birthday speech or to present an informative topic in the workplace.

This book will not teach you the art part. You have your own natural style, whether you are aware of it yet or not. This style will shape how you craft your speeches and how you deliver them. You will discover on your public speaking journey your own artistic speaking flair. It will be up to you to identify and develop this as you see fit in the context of the structures set out in this book. It will be up to you to do the work too. This book will give you advice, ideas and suggestions but it is your responsibility to apply them as appropriate to your unique speaking event.

You are now beginning your journey. I hope you are excited; you should be, you are about to embrace the life-changing power of public speaking. In the next five chapters we will break down the key elements of any successful talk. Each chapter concludes with three main take-aways and some top tips for you to use.

Putting all of this together and applying it, as we shall see, is the key to success. Well done for having the courage to embark on this journey – let's begin.

STEP 1
Concept

WHATEVER TYPE OF SPEECH YOU
PLAN TO GIVE FIRST THING IS FIRST;
YOU WILL NEED PURPOSE.
IN FACT YOU WILL NEED TWO – A
GENERAL AND A SPECIFIC PURPOSE

General Purpose

Typically the general purpose of your speech will fall into one of five categories:

- **To *inform*** – educate the audience on a particular topic, project or report or give them new knowledge

- **To *persuade*** – get the audience to accept your line of thinking and act in a certain way, for example to buy a particular product, change their lifestyle or vote for a political party

- **To *instruct*** – give the audience the necessary skills to perform a specific task or role, for example undertake a new task, bake a cake or perform first aid

- **To *entertain*** – amuse the audience through humour, dramatics or storytelling

- **To *inspire*** – encourage the audience to achieve lofty or noble goals, for example to strive towards a great challenge or to change the direction of their life

You will notice that each of the above categories is about the impact on the audience. Ultimately public speaking is not about you, but about them, and ensuring that you consider everything you say or do from the perspective of the audience will enable you to maximise the effectiveness of your speech.

Determining your general purpose will help you create the best possible content and delivery in order to reinforce the main aim of the speech. You should be able to place your speech into one of these five categories.

For example, if you will be telling the audience about your latest research findings, the general purpose is to inform. If it is a pitch for new business, the general purpose is to persuade. If you are training a bunch of new recruits to your company, the general purpose is to instruct. If it is a wedding speech the general purpose is likely to be to entertain the audience (whilst saying some flattering/unflattering remarks about the happy couple in the process of course). If you are enthusing your audience to change their lifestyle to help tackle climate change or improve their fitness, the general purpose is to inspire.

Specific Purpose

The specific purpose is the objective you want to achieve in the speech, for example to give your colleague a proper send off on their retirement, present an award or prize or introduce a new product to a client. You should be able to articulate your specific purchase succinctly and ideally in a single line. As we have already discussed public speaking is about the audience, not the speaker, so the specific purpose should reflect the impact you want to have on them. Rather than introducing a new product to client, for example, it might be to educate the client on the new product and entice them to buy it. This is a subtle shift in emphasis that will have major impacts on how you should construct and deliver your speech.

To help you hone your specific purpose you may wish to think about the six W's: who, what, when, where, why and whereby (how).

- **Who** – Audiences vary in their background, wants and needs. To give an effective speech it is important to align your style and content to your audience and keep them at the forefront of your mind. Spending a lot of time exploring technical arguments or complex mathematical trigonometry is unlikely to be meaningful to a group of hospital nurses. Similarly, the way you construct a speech for a group of teenagers will vary from that for a group of retirees. If you are using examples, these must be relevant to the audience. The size of the audience will also have an impact. When thinking about the audience it always helps to put yourself in their shoes. If you were them, what type of speech and delivery would you most like to hear? This is a useful starting point.

• **What** – the occasion will influence the nature of the speech. A social occasion such as a wedding, a birthday party or retirement will lend itself to a more causal and humorous specific purpose whilst a business pitch will be more formal. The *'what'* will also dictate the format of the speech which must be suitable within the speaking restrictions of the occasion. If it is a specialist business conference, for example, you can be more technically detailed in your speech.

• **When** – different times of day lend themselves to different types of speeches. A pre-lunch speaking slot may not be the best time for heavy technical analysis whereas an early morning event may not be the most suitable time for extolling the benefits of sleeping in late. Evening speeches at a party or a post-conference dinner will also create a particular set of influencing factors, especially if audience inebriation may be a factor. If that is the case keeping the speech short, sharp and entertaining will be advantageous. Another aspect which may be relevant if there are other speakers is the running order i.e. when you are speaking in relation to them.

• **Where** – the location will impact on the type of topics that are most suitable. Advocating for atheism whilst presenting in a church, for example, may be inappropriate. A more informal venue like a house or a bar may suit a more personal speech. That type of speech may not work so well in a large auditorium or a corporate boardroom which will require other strategies to best connect with the audience. The where is important.

- **Why** – why is your speech meaningful to the audience? Why should they care? What impression do you want to leave them with? Imagine your audience completing a feedback slip after your speech and being asked for the key take-away, what do you want them to write? Once you identify the why, it will bring clarity and direction to your speech. Make sure this is about them, not you! Avoid looking for praise or positive feedback (i.e. feedback that you were a great speaker), instead focus on the message you want to leave them with or the action you want them to take.

- **Whereby (how)** – the manner in which your speech will be delivered needs thought. Are you to give a PowerPoint presentation? Will there be a podium? Will there be a microphone? Will you be standing in front of the audience or hidden behind a lectern? All these factors will shape your delivery. Try to gather as much information on the whereby as you can ahead of time – as far in advance as possible. Visit the venue and practice if you can. Not only will this help you prepare, but it also offers you the opportunity to change some of these aspects to help you give a more effective speech.

Action 1: brainstorm some ideas around the six W's for your speech using the structure below. To help guide you, I have included two examples from my own speech preparations.

Brainstorming matrix – the 6 W's

The W	Considerations	Implications for the specific purpose
Who	Age, gender, ethnicity, nationality, experience, background, skills, knowledge, motivations	What language should I use? How detailed should I be? What examples will be most relevant? How can I best ensure engagement with my message?
What	Occasion/event	What is the purpose? Is it formal/ informal? What are the audience expectations?
When	Time of day/week/ month, position in the running order	What is the likely attention span of the audience? Am I opening or closing the event?
Where	Location	Will this impact my topic? How will it influence my subject matter or delivery?
Why	The message	Why is my speech important for the audience? Can I describe in one sentence what I want the audience to take-away?
Whereby (how)	Delivery mediums e.g. PowerPoint, microphone, podium, lectern	What media will be available? What speaking style/structure will work best?

Example 1: Wedding speech

General purpose: to entertain

Specific purpose: a personal speech which explains why I want to marry my wife and flatters her.

The W	Considerations	Implications for the specific purpose
Who	Approximately 100 friends and family members. This will include the Hungarian-speaking family of my wife. Not all guests will know our history.	Accessible to a mixed audience of ages/ backgrounds/ nationalities, include Hungarian references. No inappropriate language. Non-threatening audience.
What	My wedding	Informal style. Freedom to deliver the speech as I best see fit for the occasion.
When	Afternoon speech following lunch, before the father of the bride. Most guests will have been drinking.	Pithy speech including much self-deprecating humour to maintain engagement.
Where	A marquee at in my mother's house	Informal environment – personable speech. Potential for anecdotes.
Why	Flatter my wife, demonstrate my love and educate the audience on our history	I want the audience to understand why I love my wife. Using personal stories and reflections will be powerful.
Whereby (how)	Standing at the front of the crowd, no stage, microphone, no PowerPoint	Likely to lend itself to a speech without visual aids
Conclusion	Create a sharp, humorous speech full of warmth and personal stories elevating my wife. Casual, off-the-cuff delivery style with a decent cadence to maintain audience attention. Assume limited knowledge of our history and refer to Hungarian language/culture.	

Example 2: Work-related speech

General purpose: to inform
Specific purpose: deliver an update on the UK commercial real estate market and encourage the audience to invest using my company.

The W	Considerations	Implications for the specific purpose
Who	Real estate professionals. Large audience of 200-250 people	The audience will have an existing understanding of the industry and terminology/jargon.
What	Real estate conference	Technical analysis/opinion will be expected that can broaden the knowledge of attendees. The speech should include new knowledge/insight.
When	Mid-morning session after coffee break. Other presentations will precede and proceed it.	Audience is likely to be attentive. The context to the presentation will have been established so I can concentrate on my expert area. Opportunity to differentiate myself from other presents through humour/speaking style given that such conferences usually comprise relatively dry formulaic deliveries.
Where	Conference venue	Suitable speaking arena with access to supporting equipment as needed.
Why	Deepen audience understanding of the UK commercial real estate market, demonstrate my knowledge, and by extension my company's knowledge, of the topic	I want the audience to understand how the UK commercial real estate market works and why it represents an attractive investment opportunity. I want to implicitly promote my company leaving the impression that we are well informed and knowledgeable.

Whereby *(how)*	Elevated stage with presentation relayed in real-time on TV screens, full range of supporting audio- visual equipment available	The presentation can be supported by PowerPoint visuals which will convey significant information and add to delivery effectiveness. Presence of voice amplification means I can concentrate on material and content rather than voice projection.
Conclusion	Deliver a detailed, technical speech on the UK commercial real estate market using supporting PowerPoint material. Inclusion of appropriate humour in small amounts could enable my speech to stand-out from other presenters	

Have you completed your matrix yet? If yes, well done! You have accomplished the first step towards mastering your speech and you have set yourself up to succeed. You will have already done more thinking and preparation than most presenters on how you can effectively deliver your speech.

If you haven't completed it yet, do it now! Don't delay. You can never over-prepare for a speech; you can never start too early. If you don't have all the information right now, no problem. Complete what you can based on what you have available and add the rest in later. You'll be surprised how helpful this step is to get you thinking about your speech and setting you on the path to ensuring it is powerful. Once you take the first step momentum will build by itself. Start now.

Recap: Step 1 – Concept

• You must decide on the general and specific purpose of your speech. Your general purpose will fall into one of five categories. Your specific purpose is the objective you want to achieve.

• Thinking about the 6 W's of your speech: who, what, when, where, why and whereby (how), will help you clarify your specific purpose. It will allow you to reflect in more detail on how you should structure and deliver your speech to make the biggest impact on the audience that you can.

• Remember that public speaking is about the audience, not the speaker. Make sure that the general and specific purpose is about the them and how you can most effectively give them real value, not about you. Think about the impression you wish to leave them with.

Three top tips

1. It is never too early to start thinking about your speech and writing down your thoughts. You cannot overprepare – start now.

2. You should be able to summarise the main message/key take-away in one sentence. Tie all your planning and delivery back to your message/key take away.

3. Do not feel embarrassed to reach out to the host or organiser of the event to clarify more detail on their expectations and the specifics of the speaking arena. This will make you more prepared and it will help avoid unexpected surprises.

STEP 2
The Writing Process

CONGRATULATIONS!
YOU HAVE COMPLETED STEP 1.

YOU ARE CLEAR ON WHAT YOU WANT TO
ACHIEVE WITH YOUR SPEECH AND HOW BEST TO
GO ABOUT IT. NOW YOU NEED TO GET TO WORK
WRITING IT. YES WRITING – USING A PEN AND
PAPER OR A KEYBOARD AND COMPUTER. WRITING
DOWN IDEAS AND CONTENT IS A FANTASTIC
WAY TO STIMULATE THE CREATE PROCESS AND
MAXIMISE THE POWER OF YOUR SPEECH

As my old scout master used to say, if you fail to plan, you plan to fail. He was absolutely right and nowhere is that truer than for public speaking. The writing process is where you plan to master your speech and with a solid script, you are well on your way. This part requires time though – the more the better. Now it is time to start writing regardless of how far away your speech is. Remember, you can never over prepare.

A word on stories

Before getting into your speech structure, let's talk about evolution. Not the evolution of your speech but the evolution of humanity. Humans are a product of storytelling. We have been telling stories ever since we had the ability to talk, indeed much before we could talk through hand gestures and actions. Scientists have credited the ability of humans to tell stories as a critical factor, possibly the main factor, in our species achieving such dominance over all other animals. If you think about it all our shared beliefs are epic stories, whether it is religion, the story of nations, the story of capitalism - even the story of life itself. Once stories were told around campfires using word-of-mouth, today they are told in books, on websites/ social media or in meeting rooms or social settings. Whatever their form we are creatures of stories and we are enamored by then.

What relevance does this have to your speech? Good question. There are two implications. Firstly, the act of your giving your speech or presentation is something you were born to do. Speaking is not some innate talent that some people have and others do not. We all have it. We may just need a like advice or guidance to help us bring it out. You come from a longline of ancestors who told stories for tens of thousands of years. It is in your blood. You were born to give this speech and you are fulfilling your density by doing so. Let that thought comfort you.

Secondly, your speech is another story. On the face of it, it may seem like a work presentation, a few words at a retirement or birthday party, but in fact you are taking the audience on a journey by telling them a story. Perhaps it is the story of your product and why it is good for costumers. Perhaps it is the story of the retiring boss and why he will be missed. Perhaps it is the story of why you want to marry your wife. Whatever it is, it helps not to think of it as a technical presentation or a timeline of events but rather a story. This mindset should touch every aspect of your speech from the content to the structure to the delivery. If you read or watch any great speech, you will see that it is the speaker's ability take the audience on a journey with a story that makes it so impactful.

Rather than giving a best mans' speech, you are telling the story of the groom's quest to where he is today. Rather than giving a marketing pitch, you are telling the story of your product. Rather than giving a technical update, you are telling the story of your company finances.

Consider how the arc of your story will play out over the course of your speech. For example, a common speech story arc is the hero's journey. Strictly speaking there are 12 steps to the hero's journey but in simple terms the hero (usually the speaker) embarks on a noble pursuit, things get challenging on the way but eventually they triumph over adversity. Think about how you want the arc of your story to play out over your speech.

Structure

Whatever your story is it will need an introduction, a main body and a conclusion. All of these are very important so let's look at each in turn.

The Introduction

Introduction originates from *introductionem* in Latin. It is the act of bringing into existence. In the context of your speech you can think of the introduction as setting the stage for your story. Depending on the objective of the speech some things you may want to consider include:

• Thanking the master of ceremonies/chair and the host organisation
• Acknowledging the audience
• Introducing yourself
• Outlining the speech purpose
• Laying out the structure
• Explaining why it is important

Not all these considerations well be relevant to every speech, but to ensure you cover all bases it is always worth reflecting on and if necessary rejecting these when planning your introduction.

The introduction is an excellent time to include appropriate humour if it fits into the speech. If the audience laughs, it will help to put you at ease and you can carry that momentum with you throughout the speech. It will put them at ease too and help them to warm to you instantly.

Personal anecdotes can also work well at the start of the speech. These satisfy the natural curiosity of the audience about you. Done well they are a good way to assist the audience connect and engage with you from the outset. If you can combine an anecdote with humour – even better! This does not have to be about the speech topic itself – a comment about your journey to the conference or a memory of the venue/city you are in will do the trick.

An attention-grabbing introduction usually works well. As well as an emotive or captivating anecdote and the use of humour, try to think of other ways you can surprise or shock the audience, evoke their sense of intrigue for the content of your speech or otherwise get them to buy in to your story from the outset. Bill Gates famously released a jar of mosquitos on stage at the start of his famous talk on malaria – to gasps from the audience. What a great opener to get their engagement!

If you need to present regularly it is beneficial to have a few pre-prepared humorous openers in your back-pocket which can be applied to any situation. You can then refine these by repetition through trial and error to make them funnier and more effective based on the reactions that you get. For example, you could come up with a joke about how nerve-wracking you find presenting or a reflection on your profession and use it regularly. This is what comedians do. They road test and refine their material multiple times to determine what works and what does not to order to arrive at the most impactful delivery.

A note on humour

Humour can be your best friend when speaking in public. Appropriate, suitably timed and pitched humour is engaging and uplifting. For the speaker it helps ease tension and engender warmth and memorability from the audience. Especially in a pressured situation like a business pitch or at a large conference, humour can be immensely beneficial. It is for this reason that so many professional speakers work hard on developing their humorous abilities.

Remember that humour is not just about jokes, it comes in many forms. It can be through a play on words, a facial expression or pure tonality. Effective forms of humour include metaphors, gross exaggeration and misdirection. Public speaking lends itself to self-deprecating humour which is accessible to the entire audience and minimises the potential to offend them, given it is at your own expense. You may not believe that you are a humorous person at all but, just like public speaking, there are rules behind humour that anyone can learn. Anyone at all, including you. It is worth investing some time educating yourself about humour to help support your public speaking. You could even consider enrolling in a stand-up comedy course to learn the basics.

The Main Body

This is the meat and potatoes of your speech. Or, if you are vegan like me, the tofu and potatoes. It is the majority of your speech where you will achieve your purpose. As with public speaking itself it is useful to break this down into sections. Note down the key points you want to make. Think about the structure and how best it can be ordered to achieve your general and specific purpose. Once you have determined your order, you can build out the content by adding all the aspects you want to cover in each part.

The remainder of this section details some devices and pointers to consider when crafting your content. Only you know what you want to say so it is up to you to apply these as you see fit.

Storytelling

As you are now aware, it is useful to view your speech as if you are telling a story. With that in mind, bringing real life personal stories or anecdotes into your narrative is effective. Why? Firstly, these are already stories so they fit the story-telling philosophy exactly. Secondly, stories help to personalise you to the audience. They enable the audience to see you as a person with feelings and emotions rather than just a speaker. Thirdly, they will help to satisfy the natural human curiosity that the audience will have about you and which will aid engagement. Finally, personal stories can reveal vulnerability about you which will endear you to the audience.

Try to look for ways to include personal stories in your speech. They must be suitable for the audience though and for the environment so choose your stories wisely.

A note on timing

Be mindful of your allotted speaking time, double-check this with the organiser if you are unsure. Having acute awareness of this will help keep your content focused. It is no use planning to recount your entire life-story in intimate detail if you only have five minutes to talk. If there are no set speech timings, for example an after-dinner speech, you need to create your own timing target which is appropriate to the setting and the event and, crucially, stick to it. Usually shorter is better.

Time and again I have seen speakers at industry conferences or in pitch meetings run over their allotted time. I have seen speakers at social events deliver a fantastic speech to start with but to go on for so long that the audience goes from thinking *"what a great speech"* to *"when will this end"?* Over-running your allotted time is extremely bad etiquette and you should strive to avoid it unless it is absolutely necessary (which it rarely is).

Running over time takes speaking time away from other speakers or meeting participants. Speaking for too long when there are no definitive timings diminishes the power of your speech and audience interest in it. You are taking up more of their precious time. Sure, they may all be enraptured by what you are saying but on the off chance that they are not, respect them by keeping to time.

In addition to showing respect to the other speakers and the audience, keeping to time will also make your speech more impactful. It will force you to keep your content tight, to cut out superfluous material and to refine your key messages. Doing that will make those messages more memorable and land with greater gravitas.

When you prepare you must practice and time your speech. If you think you might run over, strip out some content. More often than not you will speak faster on the day than you do in your preparation but regardless of that, ensure that the speech you have prepared comes in at or under time in your practice sessions. That will also allow you flexibility to incorporate off the cuff remarks, audience engagement or other unplanned events on the day whilst still keeping to time.

Keep your speech as short as possible whilst ensuring you cover the main points. The attention span of a typical human is limited, even when they are listening to a great speaker, and more time does not equal more value. The maximum length of a TED talk is 18 minutes but the best speeches are often much shorter than that. A great wedding speech or business pitch of seven minutes is likely to resonate stronger than an equivalent speech of 20 minutes. Ironically the shorter the speech, the longer it takes to prepare for it so speakers who can effectively deliver short, sharp, impactful speeches have done significant work in advance.

One of my all-time favourite quotes is that of attributed to former US Presidential Woodrow Wilson. When asked how long he took to prepare a speech he responded *"It depends. If I am to speak ten minutes, I need a week for preparation; if fifteen minutes, three days; if half an hour, two days; if an hour, I am ready now."* Be like Woodrow Wilson.

A note on writing

In my experience writing out your speech content produces significant benefits, especially for less confident speakers. I have delivered hundreds of speeches over the last decade and for every single one writing out my speech has been an essential part of my preparation.

There are two main approaches towards preparing written content for speeches. One approach is to write content out word for word; the other is to write down key bullet points only. There are pros and cons of each approach.

Writing your speech out word for word ensures that you have oversight of every single aspect of your verbal content. It can allow you to better time your speech to fill your allotted slot. It also means you may be better able to plan vocal devices like pauses, volume and inclination or physical devices like hand gestures or stage positioning (more on those later). The main downside is that it can lead to a mechanical delivery in which you are just reciting your speech from memory (given you will not be using notes – again more on that later). If you forget a line or two, say it in the wrong order or mix it up it can be extremely disrupting to your flow.

Using key bullet points only will help you deliver a more natural-sounding speech. It may help to build more audience engagement, ingrain greater flexibility and preserve adaptability making it easier to tailor your speech to specific environment you find yourself in on the day. This is because you will not have set lines to recite, just key points you want to cover in a certain order. One drawback is that it may be harder to remember all the content you want to include. Another is that it could be harder to keep to your allotted time as your delivery has more potential to vary from what you have practiced and you may be prone to more waffling. This approach also needs confidence, which is why in my experience it is usually more advanced speakers who prepare in this way.

A middle ground is a combination of the two approaches. Start by writing your speech out word for word but as you practice and refine it, you can condense your notes into fewer and fewer bullet points. As a minimum though, it may help to write out and memorise your introduction and conclusion word for word. Because these are short and create the first and last audience impressions, you want to do these well. Memorising the exact content word for word may help ensure you do that. That is particularly true for the introduction. If, like me, your mind sometimes freezes in fear at the start of your speech, having a well-practiced introduction which you can deliver on autopilot will calm your nerves and get you into a more relaxed state whilst making sure that whatever happens on the day, your speech will get off to a great start.

The rule of three

A powerful tool to use when speaking is the rule of three, whether that is three distinct sections, three main take-aways, or three key observations.

Why is the rule of three so effective? The brain loves patterns and it is constantly seeking them out. Three is the smallest number required to make a pattern and for that reason, framing content in threes is an excellent way to convey complex ideas effectively. Of course you can go for more than three points but doing so commonly dilutes their potency and impairs the ability of the audience to absorb the information. Next time you listen to an effective speaker or one that resonates with you, listen to see if they are grouping content into threes. The chances are high that they are. Three is indeed the magic number.

Try to group your content into three, saving the most important or the most humorous point to last. Even if you have more than three points to make, try to be inventive to bring the rule of three into play. For example, you could include three subpoints or you could recap after each three points.

The Conclusion

A great speech needs a great conclusion. This is your space to bring your speech to its climax. What this entails will vary depending on the type of speech you are delivering but typically it will include briefly summarising your main points, preferable using the power of three or giving a call to action. You should allude to themes permeating through your speech. Often ending on a positive note, a note of urgency or incorporating humour will work well and leave a lasting impression.

What is a call to action? It is a clear instruction for the audience to act on the basis of what you have presented. It might be to buy your product; it could be to apply the life-skills you have advocated or to invest in a certain way. It could even be a call to action for yourself, for example by choosing to marry your wife! Having a call to action which neatly reflects the crux of your speech is an excellent device.

It will also be necessary to hand back control of the floor to your host or the next speaker. If possible shake their hand. In the public speaking world, shaking hands with the host or speaker before you and the one that follows signifies the power transfer of stage ownership. This is crucial, but so often overlooked.

If you are the last speaker, make it clear that this is the end of the speech or speeches. You might say something like *"that's all for today folks, please enjoy the bar!"*, *"goodnight and safe journeys home"* or simply *"see you next year"*.

One thing you should avoid doing is thanking the audience. The mindset you should have is that you are recounting to them an exciting story or educating them on an important topic. You have put hard work and a lot of time into preparing it. The speech is for the audience, not you. They should be thanking you! If you write a report or a story, you will rarely expect the author to thank the reader for reading it. It is the same philosophy for speaking. You can thank the host, the venue or the organisers, but never the audience.

A note on toasts

Many readers of this book may want to end their speech with a toast, especially if they are delivering a wedding speech, a birthday speech or a retirement speech. With that in mind it is useful to consider toasts in more detail. This knowledge is always great to have in your repertoire anyway in case you are asked to give one at short notice.

Typically toasts are given at drinks events or after dinner when the attention span of the audience is likely to be challenging to maintain for a long period. Keep your toast short. Focus on the main point or points you want to cover, ideally three points max. Cover them succinctly. Make sure your content is entirely directed to the object of your toast – be that a person, an organisation or an event. Most toasts will be joyous occasions and thus you should keep it light.

Personal anecdotes can be a great way to achieve these objectives and usually you should add humour too. Make sure any anecdotes revolve around the subject of the toast, not you. For example, at a company anniversary event an anecdote about how much the company has grown by recalling the first tiny office you worked at compared to the global presence it has today is about the subject. An anecdote about how your career has progressed at the company or how impressed your family are that you work there is about you. This type of anecdote would be very appropriate if you are the subject of the toast but not if the company is the subject of your toast. This is subtle difference which you should look out for as it may be easy for you, as the speaker, to miss.

Visually, it works well if you can have a glass in your hand whilst you give you toast. The ending of your toast should always be the same. *"Please be upstanding* [wait for the audience to stand up], *charge your glasses* [raise your glass into the air and wait for the audience to do the same] *and drink a toast to...* [the subject of the toast]. [After you announce the subject, drink from your glass and wait for the audience to do the same]. *You may now be seated".* Job done!

The review process

Reviewing, editing and refining your speech is an essential part of the speech writing process. This will hone your content to ensure the narrative is as consistent and compelling as possible. Pay particular attention to the following aspects during your review:

Language – this covers both the words you use and the way you say them. Typically the way in which we write is very different from the way we speak. For example, you may write that *'you do not enjoy public speaking'* but you may say *'you don't enjoy public speaking'.* This is a minor difference, but an important one. We tend to write formerly, using longer words and phrases compared to the more informal way in which we speak. Your written script will be said out loud so make sure you write in the manner in which you will actually say it. Try to avoid using overly long words or technical jargon if you can, even if you are presenting in a work setting. Speaking plainly will increase the ease with which your audience can process your words. Keep it simple.

Grammar – as with your language, when writing out your speech you should use grammar in the way you will delivery it. Brackets have no place in speech writing so do not use them unless they signify some other non-verbal action you want to take like pacing around the stage or using hand gestures. If you plan to take a breath or pause, put a full stop. If it is a longer pause, mark it with three full stops or whatever other punctuation works best for you. If you are expressing surprise at the end of your sentence, include an exclamation mark. Include punctuation and grammar in the way you will say it.

Content value – identify which parts of your speech are high value, medium value and normal. High value parts are those that will have the most impact on the audience – a shock perhaps, a fantastic joke or a call to action. Medium value material is that which is important but is not the speech crescendo. Normal parts of your speech are self-explanatory; normal and not heart-racing. Generally you will want to spread medium value content throughout your speech and place high value content strategically for maximum impact at the start or end of each section or topic. This will help you position your speech components for optimum effect and will keep you focused on improving parts of the speech that may lack medium or high value content. It will also help to maintain audience engagement throughout with a variety of content types. All speeches will include high, medium and low value parts. It is the way they are enmeshed that creates a great speech. There are no hard and fast rules here, experiment yourself to see what works best.

Vocal elements – we will run through the main vocal elements that you can use in the next chapter. You should also mark these in your written text. If you plan to slow down for a particular sentence, signify that with a colour or by using italics. If you plan to speak more softly, reduce the font size or if you plan to speak loudly use capitals. You can include vocal elements using brackets too or whatever works for you. If you plan your vocal elements and reflect them in the script, it will aid your preparation.

Movement – include in your script any detail on where you plan to incorporate movement. This might be stepping forward to emphasise a key point. It may be moving across the stage to a new speaking position when you progress onto a new section of your speech. Perhaps it is bringing in a hand gesture or a mime to coincide with a sentence. We will explore movement in more detail later but think about and reflect this in your written script.

Jokes – mark where you will include jokes in your script. You will want to pause after you crack a joke to allow the audience time to process it and laugh. This can be challenging because it may take a few seconds for them to get it and those seconds will feel like minutes or hours to you. Be confident, if you have a good joke the laughter will come and if no-one laughs it does not matter, just carry on as if nothing happened. The audience will not notice. Plan to have a longer pause after your jokes.

Flow – perhaps the most important aspect to consider when reviewing your script is flow. It should fit together nicely in a continuous narrative. If sections do not gel together in your script or they feel disjointed, they will not gel together when you say them out loud so make sure flow is ingrained and the speech works as a single holistic piece.

The level of detail you go into in these areas will reflect the importance of the speech. For a wedding speech which is really, really important it will be more detailed than a regular market update to a small group of clients. You will need to decide how detailed you want to be. Thinking about the importance of the speech assists with this.

The value of feedback

Having a trusted friend, colleague or mentor review your script and give feedback is immensely valuable. Ask for positive and negative feedback. As you are opening yourself up to constructive criticism this is daunting, especially if the content is very personal, but the importance of a second (or third) pair of eyes viewing your written script from the audience perspective cannot be understated. You are inherently biased when you review your text because you know what you are trying to say. However, this is not necessarily what you have written down and it may not leave the impression you want with others. An honest reviewer will let you know what will actually be heard by the audience. You can then refine it accordingly for maximum impact.

Example 1: Wedding speech

Component	Objective
Introduction	• Anecdote(s) to set the scene • Thank attendees • Heavy use of humour to engage the audience and help me feel more relaxed
Main body	Loose structure to help the speech sound informal and off the cuff, built around three sections: **4. Past** – information on how we met to inform and entertain, why we hit it off, anecdotes, self-deprecating jokes. Many audience members will not know of our history so I should assume minimal knowledge **5. Present** – how we live today, our lifestyle, comment on the wedding day itself **6. Future** – our plans for the future, starting a family, moving overseas
Conclusion	Short, succinct conclusion which ends the speech on a high note with humour

Speech extract

> # Legend
> **High value content**
> *Medium value content*
> Normal speech
> **.** = short pause
> **...** = long pause

This morning I woke up and I realised ... **wow, I'm married!** [hold up ring finger]. She actually said I DO! [upper inflexion, louder, big smile]. That was quite a momentous realisation and I pinched myself to check I wasn't dreaming.

Thank you ... ladies, gentlemen and others. It's great to have so many witnesses here to verify and bear testimony that it actually happened, and... [upper inflexion then pause] to prevent Viv from running away... [wait for laughter]. Thank you all for being here to share this special moment.

You've all heard of love at first sight?...A couple locks eyes for the first time [point to my eyes and point to hers during this section] and falls deeply madly in love? **That is NOT** (louder to emphasise word) what happened...Like all the best romances it was a slower and steadier process.

We did the modern thing, meeting online via the work messaging system at our old company. *She was in Brisbane and I was in Sydney* (upper to lower to upper tonality). That was followed by a healthy dose of Facebook stalking, I'm not gonna say by who. It must have been my profile picture that impressed her. **I was only wearing these [produce speedos from my pocket and hold them up]...my Bondi Beach Surf Lifesaving Club speedos...clearly it was these that did it [toss speedos into the crowd]** ... A few work meetings and a bit of persuasion later, she managed to entice me to visit her. I look a leap of faith and I flew to Brisbane for our first official date.

We clocked up a lot of airmiles after that tripping up and down between Brisbane and Sydney, until we'd collected enough to come back to the UK. One minute were on the beach in Bondi, **the next we were in a dingy flat in London reminiscing about the beach!** [speed up pace here] ... [pause for laughter]

Example 2: Work-related Speech

Component	Content
Introduction	• Thank host • Anecdote – pre-prepared joke about traveling to the conference • Establish creditability – brief outline of my experience i.e. what qualifies me to talk about this topic • Format of the speech – what I am going to say
Main body	**Overview** – market background and scene-setting for the UK property market **What** – major structural and market-based trends in the sector, using evidence including colour graphs displayed on PowerPoint **The opportunity** – outline an investment strategy to maximise market potential **Note:** the above structure will be used for each of the UK's four main commercial real estate markets – offices, industrial/logistics, retail, residential
Conclusion	• Summarise the three main points • Call to action – invest in the manner I have described • Hand back to host

Speech extract

Action – *click to next slide and walk to left side of stage*

Slide 41: Holding slide – picture of a logistics warehouse

Moving on to logistics [rolling hand gestures]. This has *consistently* [slow down pace] been the UK's top performer over the last few years. The sector has been re-rated and last year it delivered returns of 10.0%. **10.0%!** [higher pitch, louder]

Action – *click to next slide and walk to right side of stage*

Slide 42: Line chart showing online retail spending and online retail sales growth using Office of National Statistics data

The changing way in which we shop is the reason for this. As the Office of National Statistics data shows here [point to screen], this year online retail accounted for over 26% of all retail sales in the UK. **That is up from just 7%** [higher inflexion] a decade ago. All this means more demand for the logistics warehouse space which can fulfill online orders

This chart also shows that online sales growth is slowing...This hasn't impacted the logistics market to date. Online retailers continue to expand and existing retailers are adapting their supply chains to compete. Whilst slowing growth should be monitored, we see **strong** [louder] occupational demand for quality real estate continuing...You [point to audience] should feel confident investing in this sector....

Action – *click to next slide and walk to the centre of the stage*

Slide 43: Pie chart showing the amount of logistics floorspace leased in different locations

It is critical, **absolutely critical** [slow down pace], for logistics businesses to have fast access to suppliers, customers and labour. That explains why we have seen such strong leasing activity for urban logistics property and assets in locations with easy access to road, air or sea networks [point to slide]. We spent a lot of time looking at seaports last year given that most UK imports and exports come by sea [step towards audience]. This type of infrastructure led analysis **must guide** [louder] your investment strategy in this sector.

In summary. **Number 1 [extend one finger] logistics offers attractive returns. Number 2 [extend two fingers] online retail sales growth will support additional demand. Number 3 [extend three fingers] using an analysis that is based on infrastructure enable investment success.**

Recap: Step 2 – The Writing Process

• A great speech requires great planning. Great planning means that the speech has a strong introduction, a solid main body where you deliver your messages and an impactful conclusion. Start writing as soon as you can and use the writing process to help you clarify your thinking, refine your key messages and ensure you achieve your objectives.

• Try to think of your speech as a narrative because all of us, as humans, have evolved through storytelling. Having a strong narrative will aid audience engagement and help your message to land. Use this thinking to craft your written script and look for opportunities to tell stories within the content. Even dry work presentations should be viewed in this way.

• The writing process is about more than putting words on a page. Use this step to think about how you will deliver your words, not just what they are. You can and should plan things like pace, speed and pauses. We will explore these in greater depth in the next chapter.

Three top tips

1. Humour is a fantastic device to add life to your speech, invigorate the audience and make your message land. Identify ways to add humour to your speech. Including humour in the introduction can be particularly useful to relax the audience, and, more importantly, you! A warning though, humour should be appropriate to the audience and the occasion so you must be careful in case it backfires. If in doubt, err on the side of caution and use self-deprecating humour. Always avoid vulgar jokes whatever the occasion and never, ever, swear.

2. Your audience will have an innate fascination with you, whether they are aware of it or not. You can use this to your advantage, particularly during work-related speeches, by revealing personal details about yourself. I am not talking about your deepest secrets here or your banking card pin number. I am talking about things such as your likes/dislikes, hobbies, family situation and so on, provided it adds value to your content. Include a personal anecdote or two if you can. As well as grabbing their attention, using personal stories will make the audience more endeared to you which will mean that they are more likely to value and remember your speech.

3. You will draft, re-draft then re-draft your written script again and again during the writing process. Then, when it comes to practicing you will change it again! Do not get hung up on making your script perfect, it is merely a tool to help to you order your content, direct your practice and ensure you include devices which bring the speech to life. It is a means to an end, not an end in itself. Make it the best you can but do not let the lack of a final or perfect script delay you from moving on the next step in the process. It will never be perfect and nor should it be.

STEP 3
The Delivery

NOW YOU HAVE A WRITTEN SCRIPT, STEP 3 IS YOUR TIME TO MASTER THE DELIVERY SO THAT YOUR SPEECH HAS THE MOST IMPACT THAT IT CAN

The important of practice

Have you ever wondered why politicians give such impactful speeches? The reason is simple – practice. Politicians will travel up and down the country giving the same speech to multiple different audiences and every time they do that, they get better at delivering it. Before even thinking about a public delivery though they will have rehearsed and practiced multiple times to get it roadworthy. It may seem to you, the audience member, that this is being delivered fresh but in fact it is the product of practice, practice and more practice which is why it comes across in that way.

TED talks are another example. If you have never heard of TED talks, where have you been? I'd suggest you stop reading this book and watch a few immediately. You can watch them on TED's dedicated site and no, in case you were wondering, I have absolutely no affiliation with TED. TED stands for Technology, Entertainment and Design. Their events comprise talks of up to 18 minutes that educate or inspire the audience on diverse topics in these three areas. The best TED talks are excellent examples of mastering your speech and have been viewed millions of times. They incorporate all of the aspects I talk about in this book, especially practice. Although the speakers may look relaxed and polished on stage the typical TED speaker practices their speech 200 times. 200 times! That is why they appear so relaxed and polished.

You must adopt the same approach and practice, practice, practice. Practice as often as you can - on your commute, at home, in the shower. Practice in the speech venue if possible. Repeat your speech again and again and again, testing out different wordings and delivery devices to determine what works best. When you think you have practiced enough, practice more. This process is repetitive and it can be boring. It is usually tedious. But when the time comes to give your speech you will be thankful for every second you spent practicing and it will pay rich dividends.

Practice really is the key to success. Great speakers are great at practicing. The more you do it, the better your speech will get and the more confident you will become. I am sure you will know someone who can stand up and, without any preparation, give a good speech. Whilst this is indeed an impressive skill that a tiny, tiny minority of people possess (or claim to possess), even those people would give a better speech if they had practiced. How many times should you practice the speech? That depends on you, as an individual, and the importance of the speech. I would suggest a bare minimum of 20 times for any speech, but for important speeches this should be much higher. Clearly you cannot do that if you only finalise your script the night before. That is why careful planning well ahead of time is needed. You should look to finalise your script no later than one week before your speech but ideally many more weeks beforehand.

Notes

Your script is likely to be in long-form, but this will not be suitable for the delivery. You will have seen many presenters bringing A4 notes up to a lectern and read from them, but you will not do this as it means you are not mastering your speech. Instead you have two options - either using no notes at all or using notes effectively.

Before we consider those options, a quick word on lecterns. Standing behind a lectern and presenting places a significant barrier between the speaker and the audience. Whilst this may make the stage appear less intimidating to you as the speaker, it adversely impacts on audience engagement and it dilutes the potency of your delivery. The audience will disengage and your speech will not resonate with them as well as it otherwise would have. As you must always think about what is best for the audience, do not stand behind a lectern to present unless it is absolutely unavoidable. It is fine to place short-hand notes on a lectern and refer to them, but this would involve you standing in front of the audience and away from the lectern to present, with the lectern positioned to one-side of the stage and used only occasionally. More on this below.

No notes at all

This option is the scariest, but in my opinion there is nothing more impressive than a speaker who gives a fantastic speech without using any notes whatsoever. You can fully engage with the audience without barriers and you can use the full range of body language without the limitation of hands holding notes. It will lead to a smoother, more natural flow. Although it seems daunting, it is actually remarkably easy to deliver speeches from memory. When you are practicing, you will be repeating your speech again and again. Inevitably, your speech will become a pattern which your brain will memorise with surprising ease. The more you practice, the more the speech will become second nature and one section will flow into the next. I urge you to aspire not to use notes.

Speaking without notes requires confidence. You need to believe you can do it without notes to succeed. However, as a fail-safe mechanism you can keep a copy of your short-hand notes in your pocket in the highly unlikely event you forgot your content. I still do this every time I speak even though throughout my hundreds of public speeches I have never once needed to refer to my notes. And believe me, I am renowned for my bad memory!

An issue many speakers face when speaking from memory is that they learn their script word for word. As we discussed earlier there are two issues with this. One is that it can come across like they are just reciting their text without feeling the words or speaking them with passion. The delivery seems wooden. This can usually be avoided by practicing the speech enough that you can add the passion back in through the delivery devices which we will explore here, rather than just trying to remember the words.

The second issue is that, if they forget a word or a sentence they have written, it can throw them completely off track because they are not 'living' the speech in that moment but rather just trying to repeat the words they have learnt. To avoid this, you can refine your longform notes into shorter and shorter versions until you are left with just a few bullet points as a prompt for you to talk around. You can also deviate from your script slightly as you rehearse by changing sentences or words as you speak them. This should make you less wedded to reciting the content word for word and instead be focused on conveying the message in whatever way seems best when you are on the stage.

Using notes effectively

If you do not feel confident speaking without notes, that is fine. If notes are used effectively the impact of the speech is indistinguishable from a noteless speech. The key word is *effectively*.

Effective physical notes are not notepads, A4 sheets, iPhones, iPads or any other intrusive format held in your hands creates a barrier between you and the audience. Effective notes are either small index cards which can fit in your hand or succinct larger notes.

Index cards are probably the easier form to get right. Use them to remind you about the different sections of your speech only and to support your confidence. Do not use them to write out in detail what you plan to say - you will have practiced the speech enough to know it anyway so you will not be reliant on notes other than as a prompt. Glance at your notes as you need to but make sure you look at the audience and speak directly to them. Do not speak into your notes. Pausing to read and digest your notes before looking at and speaking to the audience is absolutely fine. In fact, it is the best way to use notes as it will slow down your delivery and help you to maintain audience connection.

Alternatively, you can use larger notes such as A4 sheets or notepads which are placed on the floor or chair in front of you, on a lectern to the side, or on a thin stand directly in front of you which allows your body to remain visible. You can then step to the side of the stage or step forward to look at your notes, remind yourself what you want to say, turn the page if necessary, then step back to the main stage and speak directly to the audience. This may feel awkward to you, as speaker, but believe it or not the audience will hardly notice. It will not negatively impact your speech in any way. To see this a masterclass on how this can be done well, see Monica Lewinski's TED talk.

I have not covered tele-prompters here. Unless you have to deliver a speech word for word due to legal or sensitively issues, avoid reading your speech off a tele-prompter at all costs. Unless you absolutely master this technique (as Barack Obama famously did), you will come across as insincere and scripted and your message will lose its power.

Vocal delivery

Vocal delivery encompasses every aspect of your speech that relates to your voice. Whilst this may sound simple there are many, many layers and dimensions to your vocal delivery, every single one of which will have an impact on how much your speech resonates with the audience.

Set out below are the main components of vocal delivery which you should be aware of. The more variety you can bring to each vocal element the more interesting and engaging your speech will be for the audience. And when it comes to critical parts of your speech – the highs, the lows, the emotional punchline – having a mind to vocal variety will maximise the impact.

Pitch

This describes the tonality of your voice i.e. how high or low you speak. In everyday life you will vary your speech constantly and without thinking as you communicate.

For example, when you ask a question you may well have a rising intonation (i.e. speak higher) at the end of the sentence. Indeed, varying the pitch can completely alter the meaning of a sentence. Think about how you would pronounce *Do it!* and *Do it?* The words are the same but the meanings are different and this is conveyed through pitch.

Four types of pitch changes will be most important to your speech
- *Rising intonation* – your voice rises as you speak
- *Failing intonation* – your voice lowers as you speak
- *Dipping intonation* – your speaking voice falls then rises
- *Peaking intonation* – your speaking voice rises then falls

Try to match the emotional content of your speech to your pitch. You should exaggerate your pitch too to make it clearer to the audience. For example, speaking in a much higher pitch to imply you are scared of something or a deeper voice to convey authority. Experiment with different pitches as you speak to see which you like best.

An extension of pitch is character voices or role-playing. These can be a very effective device if done well (or even if done badly) but are usually inappropriate for work-related speeches. For example, if you are recounting a conversation you had with someone you could use different voices for you and them. Role-playing can be highly entertaining, moving and surprising, all of which are great for the audience.

Pace

This is the speed at which you speak. Aim to speak at a conversational pace for the majority of your speech. 120-150 words per minute is a good target to ensure your message is slow enough that it can clearly be heard and understood by the audience but fast enough to maintain a decent cadence. Applying this rule of thumb to your script is a useful way to help ensure that its length matches your allotted or targeted speaking time before you start to practice. A five minute speech should be 600-750 words in total.

Try to identify speech sections in which speaking faster or slower would add to your delivery. If you want to create excitement you can speak faster, for example if you are talking about being chased or recounting an argument. Slowing down your pace will build suspense and can help ensure that important messages stand out and have a greater focus. For example, if the conclusion of your speech is to be nice to other people, consider how saying the sentence at a quarter of your speaking pace and emphasising every single word would create a stronger impact. Slowing down before the punchline of a joke or humorous sentence will also elevate its impact by creating suspense.

Power

This is your volume, how loud or quiet your voice is. Emotions such as anger and joy are suited to louder speech whilst fear or sadness is often better suited to a quieter voice. You can also play with volume to draw your audience in to key parts of your speed, such as speaking in a quieter voice if you are revealing personal information to make it sound like you are whispering the audience a secret. However you use volume, one thing you must do if you are not using a microphone is project your voice in a loud enough manner that every single one of the audience members can hear it well.

As with most aspects of public speaking, voice projection is one area in which what you perceive you are doing is unlikely to be what you are actually doing. Often speakers think they are speaking very loudly when in actuality the audience is staining to hear them. In most rooms and venues, especially one full of people, sound does not travel well so you need to over-exaggerate your vocal power to ensure that you project your voice loud enough for all to hear. You may think you sound like you are shouting but the audience will hear you at a normal volume. Try to speak much louder than you want to. Better still, position a friend at the back of the room and have them signal to you if you need to raise your voice. This is a fail-safe way to make sure you apply sufficient power to your voice.

Pauses

Pauses are integral to any speech. Use pauses of different lengths strategically timed at appropriate points in your delivery. You want a short pause between each sentence and perhaps within sentences too if your script includes a comma. You want longer pauses when you transition between sections, after you have delivered a statistic or a joke to let it sink it, or to build up suspense at the climax of your speech. You can use some really long pauses too, although doing so will require conference and practice.

If you are like most people, you will find that you speak much faster on stage than you plan to. Planning for pauses within your speech is a great way to ensure you slow yourself down and speak at a conversational pace. Practicing is critical here too ~ practice your speech in real time, pauses and all, and you will be more likely to include pauses of appropriate length on the day.

Body language

Academics have found that as much as 93% of communication is nonverbal. This makes sense when you consider that our ancestors were living together and communicating much longer than they had the ability to speak. Nonverbal communication is a basic instinct. This means that for an effective speech you must pay close attention to your nonverbal communication, or your body language.

In my experience body language is a lot easier for speakers to understand than vocal delivery because it comes naturally to most people. But in the literal and metaphorical glare of the spotlight on stage, it can often fall apart if speakers have not thought about how to use body language effectively or practiced doing so. Excellent use of body language will make a good speech great. It can also make a good speech bad if done poorly.

Outlined below are the main points to consider in relation to the body language within your speech.

Facial expressions

When you walk on stage make sure you have a big smile. Not only will this endear you to the audience, it will also make you feel more confident. Whatever your speech is about, wherever it is taking place and whatever you feel inside, start with a big smile.

Throughout your speech, try to incorporate other facial expressions as appropriate to add emotion and authenticity to your speech. Look happy when you are recounting an uplifting experience. Look serious if you are talking about a grave issue. In everyday speech you will naturally do this but when you are on stage you may not given the additional pressure speaking in public creates. It therefore helps to identify in advance where facial expressions would chime with the content of the speech so you are mindful to incorporate them and you practice doing so. As with all delivery devices, it is beneficial to exaggerate facial expressions, especially if you are giving a speech in a social setting, to add to the narrative.

Eye contact

Look the audience in the eye as much as possible. This will feel awkward and unsettling at first but do it anyway as it will magnify your connection with the audience significantly. Maintaining eye contact will make the experience feel more real to you, and scarier, which is why it is likely you will naturally try to avoid it without bringing your conscious awareness to it. To avoid eye contact most speakers look at the floor or the ceiling when they are recalling what to say next. Force yourself not to do this and instead keep your eyes firmly fixed on the audience.

Many speakers scan the audience with their eyes throughout their speech rather than picking individual members and holding their gaze. This is better than staring at the floor or the ceiling, but truly great speakers will pick audience members and hold their gaze whilst they deliver their speech. To do this, choose three or four audience members spread out around the room. Hold the first persons' gaze whilst you deliver a full sentence looking them directly in the eye. Find the second person then do the same with the next sentence. Find the third person and do the same, then the fourth. Once you have done that move your eyes back to the first person for the next sentence and repeat the process throughout the speech. The audience within the vicinity of the person whose gaze you are holding will still feel like the speech directed at them, so it will have more or less the same effect as looking everyone in the eye. It will ensure you cover the whole room with solid eye contact.

It may be easier for you to do this if you pick friends in the audience and warn them in advance. If you are speaking to a large crowd who you cannot see clearly, do the same thing with your eye contact but direct it to a different section each time. It will have the same impact.

Hand movements

As in everyday speech, your hand movements are an important part of your ability to communicate. More than that though, hand movements can be used to demonstrate confidence in your delivery and content (even if you do not feel confident).

There is no one-size-fits-all model for using hand movements, you will innately have your own style which you should try to identify and build on. Some people will naturally be more expressive with their hands, others will be more reserved. The Italians for example make heavy use of hand movements when communicating, the British far less so. It is unproductive to try to force yourself to become expressive if that is not what comes naturally to you. That said though, there are some rules which will generally work well for most people and which you should try to incorporate to maximise the impact of your delivery.

The first rule is to use some hand movement. You do not need to overthink these but do allow your hands to be free to move around and add to your speech when it is appropriate. You can plan to use some types of hand movements at certain points, such as pointing to a spot on the stage or the audience, physically counting off points on your hands, or miming parts of your speech (pretending to swig from a glass if you are talking about talking a drink, miming holding a baby if you are talking about having a child). A word of warning though, over-use of hand-movements or gestures that are too exaggerated will be distracting for the audience and adversely impact your speech. Try to include some hand gestures, but not too many, and use these as you practice to help them become ingrained.

The second rule is to free your hands. If you are to use hand movements most effectively, you cannot be holding anything at all – no notes, no microphone, no glasses of water, nothing. This is why the best speakers use head or shirt-mounted microphones rather than a handheld mic. It is another reason why you do not want to use handheld notes. With your hands free you can use them to their utmost effect to add to your vocal delivery.

The third rule is to keep an eye out for default hand-gestures that you should train yourself out of. The most common example of this is clasping your hands in front of you when you are talking. This position comes naturally to pretty much every speaker I have ever seen. The reason is that your brain believes you are physically vulnerable when you are on stage and thinks that clasping your hands together in front of you is protective by reducing the surface area vulnerable to attack (i.e. area not are). However, hand clasping or similar closed body positions create a barrier between you and the audience and convey nerves so should be avoided. There are many variations on hand clasping such as resting one hand inside the other in front of you or pressing your fingers or your palms together in front of you. Whatever the exact position of your hands and fingers if you are holding them in front of your body, it has the same effect and should be avoided.

A much better default position for your hands is to keep them firmly planted by your sides. This will feel awkward to you as speaker but it will not appear unnatural or odd to the audience. Quite the contrary in fact. To help you do this, imagine you are holding a bag of sugar in each hand which would require you to keep your hands by your side. Keep that thought in your mind throughout your speech. When you are not using hand gestures, hands by your side as if you are holding two bags of sugar.

Stage positioning

This relates to where you are physically positioned on stage and how you walk around it. Generally you will want to start and end your speeches from a central position where the entire audience can see you clearly. As you progress through the speech it will usually be appropriate to walk around the stage with purpose at logical points, such as when you transition between each section. This shows command of the stage, conveys confidence and if done well it creates a more engaging audience experience. Plan in advance when you want to move and incorporate it into your practice.

Some speakers pace the stage during their speeches. Whilst this can work well, it can also be distracting for the audience. There is a fine line between pacing enough to make things engaging and pacing too much that it gets distracting. To help you avoid crossing that line, plan in advance about when you will move around the stage and do it only at pre-planned points. Only pace or move with purpose.

Another thing to watch out for is standing too far back from the audience. It is likely you will automatically do this if you are not consciously thinking of it because you mind thinks you are in physical danger and standing further back means you have more time to react should you be attacked. That may have been a wise evolutionary trait in the past but it is not so helpful in a public speech. You are not in physical danger and standing further away from the audience creates distance between you and them, making you more difficult to see and necessitating stronger voice projection. Make sure you stand close to the audience. If you can inspect the speaking area ahead of your speech, work out where you want stand in advance and walk directly to that point before you start speaking.

Clothing

The importance of suitable clothing is often overlooked as a critical part of speech delivery. We inherently form an initial impression of someone within the first few seconds of seeing them for the first time based on their visual appearance. It is surprisingly difficult for this initial impression to be changed a later stage. You can use this to your advantage if you dress in a suitable way, but it will also work against you if you do not pay attention to it in advance.

It always amazes me how many speakers I see who are clearly well prepared, who have spent a lot of writing their speech and expended significant time and energy practicing their delivery only to let themselves down in something so easily done as dressing appropriately. Presenting in causal trousers and tee-shirt is unlikely to establish your credibility in front of a suited-and-booted business crowd; dressing in a glamourous dress in front of a casually dressed student crowd at 9am in the morning is unlikely to make you relatable to them.

As a general rule you should match your attire to the venue, occasion and the crowd. If in doubt dress a bit smarter than you think may be needed but do go overboard in case it seems contrived. Dressing suitably and dressing well in something you feel comfortable in will boost your confidence too. Whatever you do, decide well ahead of your speech what you want to wear and, if possible, wear it during your rehearsals.

Your secret weapon: filming

Public speaking distorts your perspective of time and space. The challenge with pretty much all aspects of speech delivery is to believe that you will not come across to the audience how you think you will. You may feel like you seem incredibly nervous, but the audience will not be aware of that at all if you apply the recommendations in this book. You may feel you are speaking at a normal pace, but in reality you are likely to be speaking far too fast. You may feel that keeping your hands by your sides like you are holding two bags of sugar makes you look stupid but to the audience it looks perfectly natural. This is the whole mind game of speaking. Once you understand it and use it to your advantage it is a game-changer.

One trick to help you with this is to set-up your phone or a camera to film yourself practicing your speech and watch the footage back. This is excoriating to do but given that you are focused on mastering your speech and given that this is the most effective way to understand how you are coming across in reality versus in your own head, it is a necessity. If you watch footage of yourself you will instantly see what you are doing that works well and what does not. You can then adapt accordingly. Suck up the cringeworthy-ness, watch yourself practice and you'll be amazed how fast you improve. You will also no doubt be pleasantly surprised how confident you are coming across which will be a big morale booster.

An alternative to filming is practicing in front of a mirror. This is a great technique to allow you to test out and adjust different deliveries in real time. It is especially helpful for trialing facial expressions. I tend to favour filming over practicing in front of a mirror though as it gives you a more objective impression of how the audience is likely to experience your speech and you can watch and re-watch it multiple times.

A note on ums

If you want to master your speech, you need to overcome the tendency to include ums, ahs and other similar sounds during your delivery. Next time you see a presenter in action, try to count how many ums, ahs or similar so-called 'filler' sounds or words they use including 'so', 'basically' and 'like', typically at the start of sentences or when there is a mid-sentence pause. Great presenters will have few if any of these sounds. Less polished presenters often have a very high number; indeed it is not uncommon for some presenters to include an um or ah at the start or end of every single sentence (be warned: once you start to listening out for this it is so distracting that it becomes extremely difficult to absorb anything a speaker is saying if they use a lot of filler words).

Your mind feels uncomfortable with silence when you are on stage. The way it gets around this is to fill any silent gaps with these unnecessary sounds which more often than not you may not even be aware of. However, to master your speech bring some conscious thought to this issue and do your best to remove filler sounds and words. Being aware of this issue is the first step and that alone will go a surprisingly long way towards ensuring you minimise their occurrence. Because ums and ahs occur at times when you should be silent, taking a breath when you feel an um or ah coming on is a helpful approach. Slowing down and focusing on including pauses at the end of each sentence will also assist to override your natural inclination to fill that silence with a sound.

Ums and ahs tend to creep in the most when we are on stage actually delivering our speech rather than in rehearsals. As such a good discipline to get into is to ask a friend to film you in action during the speech. In addition to being an excellent way to record your speech for posterity, watching it back will give you an unbiased way to assessing whether you need to undertake further work on your ums and ahs, as well as all the other aspects of vocal delivery and body language described in this book.

Recap: Step 3 – The Delivery

- Practice is the key to success. The more practice you do the better your speech will be and it is impossible to overprepare. Make sure you factor in sufficient time to practice well ahead of your speech and practice often.

- Vocal delivery is the way you use your voice to deliver your message. Plan which vocal devices you will use where and incorporate these into your practice.

• Body language is the non-verbal way in which you communicate with the audience. This has an important bearing on how efficiently you deliver your message and how powerful your speech will be. Think about the topics covered in this chapter, consider how you will apply these in your material and then practice accordingly.

Three top tips

1. You must override your default mental perspectives to really master your speech. Your mind will be full of self-doubt. It will be scared and think you are physical vulnerable which impacts your delivery. Trust that you will not come across to the audience how you perceive you will. Practice your delivery again and again to ingrain the tips in this chapter. All aspects of your delivery can be drilled before the main event to override your default settings. I'll say it again – practice is the key to speech mastery.

2. Film yourself practicing your speech and watch the footage back. This is excruciating but accept it will be and persevere with it because it is the best way to honestly learn how you come across. You can then make the necessary adjustments to improve your content and delivery for maximum impact.

3. Public speaking is subjective. Only you can decide how your speech should be delivered. Understanding this is empowering because it helps prevent you from agonising over the small details. If you think a particular vocal or non-vocal style is the best, you will always be right. Don't stress.

STEP 4

The Main Event

IF YOU APPLY THE PRINCIPLES IN THIS BOOK, YOU
WILL HAVE UNDERTAKEN A SIGNIFICANT AMOUNT
OF WORK IN THE LEAD-UP TO YOUR SPEECH.
YOU SHOULD FEEL WELL PREPARED AND CONFIDENT
WHEN THE BIG DAY ARRIVES, SAFE IN THE
KNOWLEDGE YOU WILL DO A GREAT JOB. THAT
WILL NOT PREVENT YOUR NERVES FROM COMING
ON AS THE DAY APPROACHES BUT IT SHOULD
AT LEAST GIVE YOU THE CONFIDENCE THAT YOU
WILL DELIVER A GREAT SPEECH REGARDLESS

On the point of nerves, I have some bad news for you – your nerves will never leave you no matter how much you practice or how many speeches you deliver. I still get super nervous every single time I speak, normally manifesting as butterflies in my stomach and an inability to concentrate, even to this day after hundreds of speeches.

You will learn to embrace the nervousness. Better yet, you will learn to enjoy it. It is your nerves that keep you sharp on the day and prevent your confidence turning to arrogance. It is your nerves that will make you put in the work needed to master your speech. Conquering your nerves is what gives you a tremendous buzz when you deliver a great speech. That buzz becomes addictive and will make you want to speak in public again.

Now you have done all the work and are primed for success, lets consider some things to think about and do on the big day itself.

In the hours before

1. **Apply positive self-talk.** When it comes to public speaking, as with most things in life, your mind can either be your greatest enemy or your greatest asset. Make sure you use it to your advantage on the day.

   If you have applied the approaches outlined in this book and you have practiced a lot, the main event is really just a formality. You have done the hard work, now is time for the payoff. Try to relax and be confident that you will deliver a fantastic speech. Really believe you will, visualise it.

   If you have not applied the approaches as much as you have liked, or you feel you should have practiced more, do not beat yourself up about it or allow self-doubt to creep in. Doubt is toxic and it serves you no useful purpose. Trust that whatever you have done is enough and concentrate on doing the best job you can through positive self-talk and visualisation. Be kind to yourself and be confident that you will deliver a fantastic speech.

2. **Practice *(a little).*** It may help to run through the content a few last times on the day of your speech. Do not obsessively practice though. The real preparation is done in the weeks and days before your speech so there is little advantage in doing too much rehearsal on the day itself. You would be better served relaxing and forgetting about it (as far as you can) so that you are in a good frame of mind when the time comes. In my experience speech practice really solidifies overnight after a good sleep – the day after you have done some solid practice you will be amazed how much of it sticks. Practicing on the day does not add much value and may make you feel more nervous or fearful. Feel free to do a few dry runs to build your confidence but do not overdo it.

3. **Familiarise yourself with the speaking area.** The more familiar you can become with the speaking area before the speech, the more comfortable you will be and the better you will be able to utilise the space to your advantage. Take the time to visit the venue early, stand on stage to get a sense of how it will feel when you are up there for real. Make a mental note of anything that might be relevant – where people will be sitting, how you will walk up to the stage, whether there are any obstructions. Under the best-case scenario you can even do a dry run or two of your speech from the stage which will be excellent preparation for the main event.

4. **Familiarise yourself with the format.** Check in with the event host to double and triple check the format. Make sure you know when and how you will be called to the stage and who you need to

pass on to when you leave. Check timings and any other relevant aspects.

5. **Check any equipment.** I cannot count how many times I have seen presenters take the stage and then suddenly discover they have no idea how to work the slide clicker or the microphone. I talked previously about how important it is to start your presentation strongly and technical issues will impede your beginning, possibly severely, which will have repercussions for the rest of the speech. It is imperative you check, double-check and triple check any equipment before your presentation and are certain how to use it.

6. **Limit/avoid alcohol.** If you are feeling anxious about your speech and are in an environment in which alcohol is flowing such as an evening dinner, a wedding or social function, it can be tempting to have a drink (or four) to calm your nerves. Do not do this. You will need the full complement of your physical and mental skills available to you for the speech and for the majority of us, alcohol will detract from that. If you feel you must indulge, limit yourself to one or at the very most two drinks. Being drunk, even mildly so, on stage is a bad look even at social events, and people will remember your drunken appearance more than the speech. I have seen this destroy reputations. Be careful.

In the minutes before

1. **Loosen up.** Your body carries tension physically so if you feel nervous, which you will, your body will tighten up and you will come across as stiff and robotic when you are on stage. To help you loosen up, physically shake yourself out and stretch your body in the minutes before you go on stage if you can. Shrug your shoulders, shake your hands, arms and legs. Not only will this

help you appear more relaxed and less nervous, it will also actually make you feel more relaxed and less nervous too.

2. **Breathing.** Another place you carry tension is your diaphragm (i.e. your stomach) and, as with your physical body, loosening it up before you take the stage is beneficial. Release tension in your vocal cords by consciously breathing from your diaphragmrather than your chest. You can let out some vocal harmony's too and beat your chest whilst you do so like Tarzan. This sounds extremely odd but trust me, it is extremely effective. It is likely that you can only practice vocal harmony's if you have privacy but deep breathing into your diaphragm can be done from anywhere, including on stage if the event has a panel-style format.

3. **Positive self-talk.** I have previously mentioned the power of positive self-talk and at no time is this more important than the minutes before your speech. You can and will be afraid. That is good, it keeps you sharp and it is the reason why you will get an endorphin rush after delivering a fantastic speech, or even a mediocre one. It is the reason you have put in so much preparation to bring you to this point. Fear is good. Doubt is toxic and you must avoid it at all costs. It serves no useful purpose ever, especially at this stage. It is entirely within your control to prevent self-doubt creeping in – do not allow it to take hold. If you start doubting yourself, apply positive self-talk and remind yourself you are practiced and ready to go. You can distract yourself by talking to guests or other speakers, re-reading your speech, getting a glass of water or any other task that will divert your attention. Accept you will be afraid, accept the butterflies in your stomach but stop that manifesting into self-doubt. Stamp it out before it arises.

4. **Stand up.** If you can, stand up before you walk on stage, straighten your dress, your suit, your tie or whatever you are wearing and start to smile. Your speech does not begin when you start speaking, it begins the moment you step into the limelight and start walking to the stage. If you are in a room or an auditorium, it helps if you can position yourself at the back of the room and walk to the stage from there. It creates a more imposing entrance and a solid walk to the front will build your confidence.

During the speech

1. **Smile.** We have talked previously about the importance to smiling, whether you feel like it or not! Constantly remind yourself to smile during your speech, it will really help how you feel and how you come across to the audience.

2. **Relax.** Being on stage can be overwhelming. Remind yourself to relax. Relax your body by leaving your arms by your side rather than clasping them, imagine you are holding two bags of sugar as mentioned before. Relax your shoulders by keep them back and down. Relax your pace and your tone. Even if you do not feel like relaxing, going through the motions anyway will have a knock-on positive effect on how you feel. Fake it till you make it.

3. **Deep breaths.** Remember to breathe, and breathe deeply, when you are on stage during the pauses in your speech. This will settle any anxiety and slow your dialogue, which is important given you will naturally speak faster than you imagine as being in stage distorts your perception of time. Breathing deeply, often, will force you to moderate your pace and help calm your nerves.

What happens if you forget your speech or freeze?

This is highly, highly unlikely to happen. If it does, the first thing to note here is that whilst forgetting your speech or freezing mid-way through will seem like a big deal to you, it is not an issue for the audience. Everyone knows how hard presenting is. The audience expects you to be nervous and if this happens, they will understand and will not judge you harshly for it. Quite the opposite in fact, they will sympathise and feel greater warmth and affinity towards you as a result so in all likelihood it will work in your favour. Even so, it is best avoided if possible. Practice is the best way to head this off, as your body and mind will usually kick into autopilot if you have practiced enough. However, if you do forget or freeze these are some tips that can help:

1. **Tell a joke.** Have a prepared joke that you can drop in if you freeze or forgot. Because this relates to specifically to the freezing or forgetting incident, the same joke will work in every situation no matter what context you are presenting or to whom. Make sure the joke is funny, really funny and make yourself the butt of it. This will make light of the situation; the audience will love it and will give you opportunity to gather your thoughts before continuing. When speakers do this well it can enhance the speech much more than a perfectly delivered speech without such an incident. For example, it might allow a light-hearted interlude from an otherwise technical and dry speech which the audience will appreciate. This is not a reason do it deliberately but it is no big deal if it does occur.

2. **Time-out.** Forgetting or freezing can rattle you and allow self-doubt to start arising. You can have a brief time-out to settle you down and give yourself the space to take a few deep breaths which

to relax you and get back into your flow. A time-out may include walking to the side of the stage to take a sip of water, checking your notes or just having an extended silence. It will barely be noticeable to the audience but it'll give you the opportunity to regroup and then continue as if nothing had happened.

3. **Back-up notes.** Keep a full-back backup copy of your notes handy in a back pocket, an inside pocket or a nearby lectern (not in your hands). If you have a complete collapse of confidence, this will allow you to continue by simply reading your notes out loud if all else fails. Clearly this scenario is not ideal but it is better than walking off the stage without finishing the speech. The audience will sympathise with you if this happens and respect your courage in remaining on stage to continue, but treat it as a fail-safe only if the above two techniques fail. As you are reading your script you may well find your confidence returns in which case you can put your notes away and carry on as if nothing has happened. If your confidence does not return, you can read the speech right through to the end.

4. **Do not apologise!** The tendency if you freeze or forgot will be to apologise to the audience. Do not do this. You are doing your best; you are trying hard and it is a stressful situation. You have no reason to apologise. The audience will empathise and apologising does nothing to resolve the situation other than implying you have done something wrong, which you have not. It may also adversely impact your confidence by changing your mindset to an apologetic one which is inappropriate in this situation. Channel the words of Winston Churchill, a great orator, who once (allegedly) said *"never apologise never explain"*. In this instance anyway, he was right. Resist the urge to apologise, it will do nothing beneficial.

A final note on nerves

Nerves will always be with you, no matter how much public speaking you do. Believe it or not you will come to appreciate them so view them positively.

As we have discussed before, having nerves is a blessing because they keep you sharp and ensures you are really in the moment. It is the experience of having nerves beforehand and successfully delivering a powerful speech regardless that gives you such a buzz and sense of self-satisfaction afterwards. The more nerves you have, the bigger the buzz! That is the reason why so many people (including yours truly) become addicted to public speaking once they learn the techniques that allow you to master your speeches every single time.

There is a trick I often use to help manage my nerves which makes the audience seem less intimating. Rather than viewing them as a mass of people to be impressed, think about the fact that every single audience member, as a fellow human being, has hopes and dreams as well as pain and suffering in their lives. They have all experienced happiness, joy, heartache, sickness, death, or they will do at some point. Have empathy for them. Get yourself into a mindset that your speech will make a positive impact on their lives and you are doing them a service by delivery it. This slightly grim but empathic perspective will give you a warmer delivery and make you feel less nervous.

A more lighthearted trick along these lines is to imagine the audience in their underwear, on the toilet or as infants or babies. Your intimidation and fear of them will soon diminish!

Stage etiquette

Whatever type of speech you are delivering, remember these two small but crucial points on stage etiquette:

1. **Shake hands.** Shaking hands with the person who introduces you is imperative. This act transfers ownership of the stage to you and signals you are now in control. If the introducer does not lead with a handshake (as they should), you can instigate it.

2. **Hand over.** Once you have finished your speech, make sure you hand the stage over to whomever follows you. If you are handing over to another presenter, make sure you introduce them, lead the applause and then shake their hand to signify the transfer of stage ownership. If you are the final or only speaker, you should round off the event in one of the ways we previously covered. Whatever you do never, ever finish with *"thank you"*. Remember that the attitude you should have is that you are doing the audience a favour by sharing your speech with them. You have no reason to thank them, they should be thanking you! In any case what are you thanking them for? For physically being present? For listening? It is a meaningless ending, avoid it. You can thank the presenter, the organisers, the staff or another specific person or entity, but do not use a generic *"thank you"*.

Recap: Step 4 – The Main Event

• Preparation on the day is vitally important. Remember to spend time in the hours and minutes before your speech getting ready and preparing yourself in the manner described here. This will pay major dividends.

- During the speech use the techniques explored in this chapter to help you relax, control your nerves and do justice to the content you have prepared. These include smiling, taking deep breaths and being empathic towards the audience.

- Ensure you know what you will do in the highly, highly unlikely even that you freeze or forgot your speech. Having a prepared joke, taking a time-out and maintaining ready access to your written notes are all ways to effectively deal with this situation should it arise.

Three top tips

1. As with life in general, smiling before and during your speech will improve the experience. It will make you feel better, it will endear your towards the audience and may well encourage smiles from them too. Smile as much as possible, the bigger the better.

2. Apply positive self-talk before and during your speech. Do not allow doubt to creep in. Beating yourself up serves no useful purpose regardless of how much preparation you have or have not done. Tell yourself only positive things and believe them.

3. Embrace your fear. Public speaking is tough which is why most people are terrified of it and why you are reading this book. You will feel fear, you will feel nervous and scared no matter how much practice you do. Be grateful for the feeling of fear in all its forms, it is what will keep you sharp and focused. It is what will give you a huge endorphin rush once you have delivered your speech. Do not try to deny the feeling, instead try to embrace it. Feel the fear and do it anyway.

STEP 5
The Debrief

GIVING A SPEECH DOES NOT END WHEN YOU WALK-OFF STAGE AND COLLECT THE ACCOLADES. A CRITICAL PART OF THE PROCESS IS THE DEBRIEF.
THIS IS THE OPPORTUNITY TO REFLECT ON YOUR SPEECH – WHAT WORKED, WHAT DID NOT, WHAT LESSONS YOU LEARNT – SO YOU CAN IMPROVE NEXT TIME

Feedback

The most important aspect of the debrief is to seek feedback. You can ask audience members afterwards what they thought about the speech on an ad hoc basis. Better still tell people in advance that you will seek feedback from them afterwards so they are paying special attention to your delivery. Getting honest, balanced feedback is key and that means understanding what worked but, more importantly, what did not work or what could have made the speech even better.

Most people will only want to give you positive feedback and most will be inclined to only remember the aspects they thought worked well. You will need to be clear that you want both the positive and the negative and be prepared to accept negative feedback gracefully without being defensive. Put your ego aside! If you have applied the guidance in this book you will have delivered a powerful, resonating speech, but there is always room for improvement. Even the best speech can always be tweaked in one way or the other – structure, language, hand gestures – to make it even more impactful.

Because public speaking is an art, not a science, feedback will be subjective. You need to use you own judgement to determine if the feedback is valid and how you should apply it, if at all. For that reason it is great to ask several audience members to review the speech so you can get a spread of feedback and determine the commonalities and differences between them. Chances are that an audience member will be a better judge of what worked well and not so well than you will be on stage so you should value their feedback highly.

Another essential source of feedback is yourself. A day or two after the speech is delivered sit and reflect on it. What do you think worked well? What could be improved? What would you do differently next time? Write this all down so you can review it well ahead of your next speech and act on it accordingly. A great way to honestly evaluate yourself is to ask an audience member to film your speech and watch the footage afterwards. Cringeworthy yes, but a truly fantastic way to become a better speaker.

Ways to develop

I hope the success of your speech will ignite within you a deep desire to take on more public speeches. That may sound farfetched now but believe me, the exhilaration that comes from conquering your fears and delivering an excellent speech is highly addictive. With that in mind, here are a few suggestions on how you can cultivate your stagecraft and your own innate speaking abilities:

- **Practice.** Public speaking is an applied skill that you learn by doing. That means the more you practice, the better you get. It will provide you with more experience, build your confidence and enable you to develop your own style well ahead of future speaking engagements. A great way to do this is to join a public speaking club which provides a safe space to practice and experiment, hone your skills and gather constructive feedback. Toastmasters International is a global network of such clubs and there is bound to be one near you. Check them out online.

- **Learn from others.** Critiquing other speakers is a fantastic way to stimulate ideas, determine what works well and consider different styles you may want to emulate. Go out of your way to expose yourself to as many varieties of public speakers as you can. You need not even leave the comfort of your own home to do this – online talks are a great median to do so. TED has an extensive and entirely free library of speeches which is an excellent starting point.

Whilst watching virtual speeches is great, being in the audience in person is even better as you can pick up on more delivery nuances and energy. Try to attend as many in-person talks, seminars or other events as you can. If you join a public speaking club there will be a wealth of opportunity to learn from others in person on a regular basis.

- **Seek out opportunities.** If you are serious about becoming an effective public speaker, you should actively pursue opportunities to speak in a variety of situations. You learn by doing so put yourself out there. Volunteer for presentations, panels, seminars or other opportunities that may arise. Let it be known at work that you are actively looking for the opportunity to speak, chances are others will be more than happy for you to take these given how much terror the thought of public speaking triggers in most people. There are inventive ways to do this too. Charities, for example, are often looking for volunteers to go out and introduce their work to various bodies like schools and businesses. Even volunteering as a group leader at your local guide or scout group will give you the chance to practice public speaking regularly, and to a tough crowd of kids too! Be inventive.

Recap: Step 5 – The Debrief

- Seeking honest feedback from several audience members after any speech is an important means through which to improve. Speak to some trusted people in advance of your speech to ask them to provide balanced feedback afterwards and make it clear that you want to know the good and the bad. Try to pick people of different backgrounds and in different physical positions to get a variety of perspectives.

- Practice, practice, practice. Take any and every opportunity to practice public speaking. This is the best way to improve. Practice as much as possible as often as possible to build your confidence, develop your skills and cultivate your own unique speaking style.

- Learn from others by attending as many in-person speeches as possible and reviewing effective (and not-so effective) speakers online. Critique these speakers. Consider what you like, what you dislike and what ideas you want incorporate into your own speeches.

Three top tips

1. Actively foster an interest in public speaking. If you enjoy the process of attending events, critiquing the speakers and watching deliveries online you will do it because you want to, not because you feel you need to, and you will reap the rewards in your speaking abilities.

2. Join a public speaking club. This will provide a supportive environment in which to try, test and develop your speechcraft. It will commit you to a regular schedule of practice and improvement.

3. Put aside your ego. This applies both when you are on stage to ensure you give the speech your best, regardless of how uncomfortable or risky it may seem, as well as when receiving feedback. No-one likes to hear anything less than extremely positive feedback but understanding which parts of your speech could be improved upon means you will do a better job next time. This can only come from hearing, accepting and responding to non-positive (i.e. neutral or negative) feedback. If you can successfully put your ego aside, rise above your internal impulse to resist negative feedback and absorb it, you stand the best chance of delivering an even more powerful speech next time.

Conclusion

Here you have it. Distilled in the pages you have just read is the distillation of my wisdom, insight and guidance on how to master any public speech gained from my years of experience watching and helping novices develop into exceptional public speakers. It reflects my personal experience too, given I was also one of those novices with a deeply held, over-powering and pervasive fear of public speaking. You CAN overcome your fears. You CAN become an exceptional speaker. You CAN gain tremendous satisfaction and career success from developing your own talents. You WILL do it if you put into practice the advice contained here.

If you apply the advice laid out in this book, you will deliver a powerful speech again and again and again. More than that, you will be on your way to discovering the life-changing, transformational power of public speaking. You will also discover the secret that public speaking is an ability anyone has and a skill everyone can learn, including you. The key though is the apply the advice. Public speaking is an applied skill that you learn by doing – so act now!

Printed by Amazon Italia Logistica S.r.l.
Torrazza Piemonte (TO), Italy

45818107R00047